Sitting Pretty

A play

Amy Rosenthal

Samuel French — London
New York - Toronto - Hollywood

SITTING PRETTY

Sitting Pretty was first presented at the Chelsea Centre Theatre on the 22nd November 1999 with the following cast:

Nancy	Yvonne D'Alpra
Nina	Judy Loe
Zelda	Amy Marston
Philip	Christopher Ravenscroft
Max	Christopher Strauli
Luka	Edward Hughes
Josie	Penny Bunton
Bridget	Tina Martin
Sylvia	Helen Blatch
Martin	Nigel Barden

Directed by Jacob Murray
Designed by Louise Ann Wilson
Lighting designed by Aideen Malone

CHARACTERS

Nancy, plump, faded, 55
Nina, slight, dynamic, 53
Max, jovial, round-faced, mid-fifties
Philip, artist, 48
Zelda, sassy, attractive, 20
Josie, brittle, elegant, 38
Sylvia, a stately lady, mid-sixties
Martin, thin, tetchy, mid-forties
Bridget, wife of Martin, mid-forties
Luka, tall, handsome,18

The action of the play takes place in a comfortable living-room of a small London surburban flat, an artist's studio and the National Gallery café.

Time: 1999

The author would like to thank Mel Kenyon, Francis Alexander and The Chelsea Centre, and David Edgar; with special thanks to Stephanie Dale and Karen Woodman

This play is dedicated to
my family
with love

Also by Amy Rosenthal
published by Samuel French Ltd

Lifelines

ACT 1

SCENE 1

The neat, comfortable living-room of a small, London, suburban flat

Left and right-hand doors indicate two bedrooms, and a central open door suggests a kitchen. There is a front door. There is a painting of Florence hanging on the wall

As the play begins, Nancy is slumped on a sofa, wearing a coat and scarf. She is fifty-five, plump and faded, with a baffled, collapsed look

The Lights come up

Nina, fifty-three, enters. She is slight and dynamic, with a sharp face and an air of fierce energy. She wears a smart suit and carries two shopping bags and a briefcase. She puts down the briefcase and carries the shopping bags into the kitchen. During the following, as she talks, she moves between the kitchen and the living-room. When she is in the kitchen she raises her voice rather than pausing

Nina What a bloody day. What a bloody marathon. I haven't stopped talking since I got out of bed. You hungry? I'm starving. I've done six tours of the entire National Gallery on a handful of dry-roasted peanuts; I'm ravenous. I was stuck so long in bloody Camden tonight I seriously considered getting out the car, leaving it in the traffic jam, doing the shopping and coming back. Anyway I squeezed into that hideous car-park, against all the odds. Chicken escalopes all right for you, tonight? (*Beat*) So then this afternoon I had these tourists. A coachload, no less, the Winnipeg Circus Skills Society, fresh from a week in Stratford-on-Avon. And this man had never heard of Constable. He said "Gee, so you Brits had an artist too?" So I asked him, very nicely, if he'd ever come across Turner, And then this woman, nose job, must have been the wife, she says, "Sure honey, you know *The Haywain*. It's the one Marcie has on her nicotine patch." I mean, Christ! It's bad enough they're selling Monet bloody mousemats in the gift shop, but a nicotine patch, I could scream! (*Beat*) Salad with this? I got baking potatoes, but I thought I might do rice. Right. Preheat the oven. I'm starving, are you?

She exits into the kitchen

A beat

She returns. She looks at Nancy properly for the first time

Why are you wearing your coat?

Black-out   Nancy exit
                         SCENE 2

The flat, as before

The doorbell rings

Nina, dressed smartly, enters from her bedroom. She crosses to the front door

Nina Hallo, Max. Come in.

Max enters, a jovial, round-faced man in his late fifties. He carries a small tray of sunflower seedlings

Max Hey, look at you. Give us a twirl! Fantastic!
Nina Mm, well, my hair's terrible. Can't do a thing with it. Sorry, Max, I'm running really late. Will you make yourself a cup of tea?
Max You just get yourself ready, Nina, don't worry about me. (*Referring to the seedlings*) Oh, this is for you, from the greenhouse. Well, it's for Nancy, but it's for you too. It's for both of you.
Nina Sweet of you, Max. She'll like that.
Max Well, it's for you too.
Nina Yes, all right. Thank you.

A slight pause. Max looks around

Max So where is that sister of yours?
Nina (*indicating Nancy's room*) Where d'you think? She's been in there for most of April.
Max But what's she doing in there?
Nina She's just lying there. Inert. Staring at the ceiling. I came in from work tonight, and I took her a cup of tea, and I put it on her bedside table. Then when I went in just now it was still sitting there. Cold, of course. I said, "Didn't you want that?" And she said "Yes, but it was too far away." *Too far away*? She only had to stretch her arm out!

Max Blimey.

Nina I know. She said she was *watching* it. The steam coming off it. She lay there and she watched it go cold. What am I supposed to say to that?

Max It's not easy for you either, situation like this. It's stressful for everyone, it's a stressful situation. You've got to think of yourself as well, Nina, you can't expect yourself to ——

During the following speech, Nancy opens her door and creeps slowly into the room, unseen by Nina or Max. She moves cautiously, like an invalid. She stops and stands still, hugging herself. She wears a cardigan over a long nightdress

Nina I mean, I get home at the end of the day, completely shattered, hoping she might at least have peeled a few potatoes, and there she is sitting on the sofa, gazing into space, wearing fifty cardigans. Or she's standing in front of the fridge eating lumps of things. Chunks of things. Cheese, chocolate, hard-boiled eggs. And pickled onions, pickled bloody onions! I can't stop her. She gets up at two in the morning and eats a full jar of the bloody things, and then she says she can't sleep! Well who *could*?

Max Comfort eating, that's what that is. Eating, for comfort.

Nina Well, yes, I realize that, but she won't be very comforted when she can't get into any of her clothes. (*Beat*) And it has been nearly a month now, Max, and I've every sympathy but, you know — worse things happen. And if we all subsided like blancmanges every time we … (*She sights Nancy*) Oh. Hallo, pet. All right? Say hallo to Max, he's brought you a plant, look.

Max Just a little something for you. Both.

Nina I should get going.

Nina exits to her room

A pause

Nancy sits, looking pitiful

Max (*gently*) I'm sorry about your job, love. Rotten thing to happen, losing your job. Makes you feel rotten. I should know. Worst time of my life, being made redundant.

Nina enters, clipping on an ear-ring

You feel useless. You feel ——

Nina Well, it's worse for Nance, in a way. Being fired.

Nancy Not fired, Nin. It wasn't firing. (*To Max*) They had to let me go.

Nina Well, let go, fired, whatever. Semantics. It's all the same. Fact is, it's an unfair dismissal. I keep telling her, Max, we could sue if she wanted.

Nancy I don't want to——

Nina She doesn't want to. But it's ageist discrimination, plain and simple. And sexist. It's very topical.

Max Can you prove that, though?

Nina The chap who sacked her ——

Nancy No, Nin ——

Nina The chap who *let her go,* Barry Cropper, her boss, he's fifty-eight. And she's only fifty-five, aren't you?

Max Now that *is* out of order …

Nancy (*sadly*) He's got a mug that says "Fifty-Eight Ain't Too Late." He has his Cup-A-Soups in it.

Nina Well, at least you're not making them any more. Right, I must dash, the traffic will be murder.

Nancy Where are you going?

Nina Oh Nance, I told you. It's an auction of fine art. I shouldn't be late, I suppose there'll be drinks and things afterwards. Will you be all right? Good. Bye, Max dear. Thanks for this.

Max escorts Nina to the door, helping her on with her coat

Max You have a lovely evening. You look a picture. (*He cautiously pecks Nina's cheek*)

Nina Well. See you later. Don't indulge her.

Nina exits

A pause

Max She looked a picture, didn't she? (*Beat*) Now. How about a nice cup of tea? I bet you could do with one, I know I could. What d'you say?

Nancy I can't seem to taste anything much, Max.

Max That's depression. You lose your senses. They do come back, believe me. I remember, I couldn't eat for weeks when Pam left.

Nancy Except pickled onions. I can taste pickled onions.

Max moves over to Nancy and sits beside her. He takes her hand

Max Nance. It's not that bad, you know, not working. (*Beat*) I mean, don't get me wrong, I know how you feel. It's rotten, being asked to leave and everything, 'specially when you've been there all that time. You feel rejected, used, useless. Like you just don't cut the mustard any more. Like you're over the hill, out of the race. Knacker's yard time.

Nancy is fighting back tears. Max doesn't notice

Thing is, though, once you get past that, it's not that bad. I mean, sure, at first it's pretty bleak. Waking up in the morning with no point to your day, no purpose. Thinking why should I even bother to get out of bed? Rest of the world rushing about, doing their business, getting on with it. Milkman delivering milk, postman delivering post. And you're standing there in the middle of the room, rooted to the spot while the hours go by. Not thinking, not moving. Turned to stone.

Nancy starts to cry quietly. Max remains oblivious

I've been there, Nance, where you are now. But I'm living proof: it gets better! Look at me! I can do all the things I ever wanted to do. Jump in the car and drive to the lakes, go fishing for a few days. Potter about in the greenhouse, come and visit Nina. And you. I can do whatever I like! And after a while, you'll get used to it, and I'll tell you something else and you'll think I'm barmy, but you'll *actually start to enjoy it.* I know you can't see it now, but I tell you, Nance, take it from me, these are going to be the best years of your life.

Nancy bursts into loud, hopeless sobs. Max, at a loss, pats her feebly. He looks desperately aroud for something to distract her. His gaze alights on the sunflower seedlings

Hey, Nancy. Nance? You see these little seedlings here?

Nancy looks up and nods through her tears

You see how they're leaning over to the left like that? Yes? Now, d'you know why that is?

Nancy shakes her head

Can't hear you, love. D'you know why?

Nancy (*snuffly*) No.

Max Well, we gardeners call that *phototropism.* Mean anything to you? No? Well, it means: growing towards the light. Now, those little fellers have been sitting in my greenhouse for the last couple of days, with the sun coming at them from the left-hand side. So they lean to the left, they gravitate to the source of light. Clever, isn't it? If you've got one lot of seedlings evenly lit, and you shine a directional light on the other lot, you'll see it happen. The ones with the directional light, they'll turn towards it. 'Cause they know they need that light to open up. They turn towards the light — and open up.

Nancy watches the seedlings, her sobs subsiding

(*Very gently*) You just have to sit out the worst bit, you know. The point where you think it's actually unbearable. It's like any pain, it's like a migraine. If you can get through the moment when you think your head's going to explode, or your heart's going to break, then I promise you, Nance, it does get better. It gets better from there on in. (*Pause; heartily*) So, I bet you're thinking, where's that cup of tea he promised me? (*Beat*) Coming right up!

Max exits

Nancy, all alone, stares bleakly ahead

SCENE 3

A dark room, which we will later recognize as an artist's studio

A raised plinth in the centre draped in material could easily be mistaken for a bed. Zelda, aged twenty, reclines there, smoking a cigarette. She wears a thin Chinese silk robe

Philip enters, forty-eight, buttoning up his shirt. He watches Zelda for a moment

Philip I have to go. (*Beat*) Zeld? I've got to go.

Zelda stares ahead of her, expressionless

Zelda Do you have any idea what you do to me, Philip? Do you have any *idea* what you do? (*Beat*) You make me feel like a hotel.
Philip A hotel?
Zelda You move in. Take up residence. Occupy my head. You move in like some ageing rocker and you storm through my corridors, trash my rooms, empty my mini-bar and check out without paying in the middle of the night.
Philip Zelda ——
Zelda Every night. What pisses me off more than anything, though, what really makes me want to *scream,* is that when you leave, when you go, when you've gone — you're still there. (*She taps her head*) In here. You're still there.

Beat

Philip Sorry.

Zelda It's not the same for you, is it? I don't live in your head. I don't fill your
thoughts. You can do what you like; read the paper; watch the news; make
a peanut-butter sandwich; whatever. Without even thinking of me. I don't
really cross your mind unless I cross your field of vision.

Philip Zelda, sweetheart, this not something we can resolve in four-and-a-
half minutes. I really do have to go.

Zelda Well *go*, then, Philip!

Philip Look, we can talk on Thursday. Will I see you on Thursday?

Zelda (*weary*) Oh, I expect so. Yeah. I expect so. (*She refuses to look at him*)

Philip moves forward and kisses the top of Zelda's head and then exits

Zelda lets out a gasp of air and hugs herself violently

Black-out

SCENE 4

The flat, as before. Several hours have passed

*Max is asleep, snoring. His jacket is draped across a chair. Nancy is sitting
on the sofa, finishing a jar of pickled onions with a fork*

*Nancy hears Nina approach and hastily pushes the jar of onions under the
sofa and puts the fork, upon which a large onion is impaled, in the breast
pocket of Max's jacket*

Nina enters, flushed

Nina (*excitable*) Hallo! What have you done to Max? Gosh, aren't I late. I
didn't realize it was so late. Well, there were some very interesting people
there. A lovely Italian lady who collects early Cezannes; and I was telling
her that I studied in Florence and it turns out that her brother was in the year
above me, graduated in '67. I remember him now. Funny eyes. Anyway
he's a rather eminent art historian now, lives in Rome, four grown-up kids.
So. How're you feeling?

Nancy Um ...

Nina Listen, I was thinking on the way back, what you need is a project. Get
you back on your feet. I was talking to a very nice lady from Guildford and
her husband's been through a terrible depression, lasted months, on
Prozac, everything. Then she persuaded him to start collecting, and he's a
completely changed man. Honestly, you wouldn't know there was a thing

wrong with him. I mean, everyone needs a project, don't they? I'd be lost without all my projects.

Nancy But ...

Nina (*sitting down*) But what?

Nancy But isn't it expensive?

Beat

Nina Oh Nancy, for heaven's sake, I'm not suggesting you do what he did, I'm just suggesting you do *something*. As a kind of variation on *nothing*. That's all. (*Beat*) Look, why don't you come in to the Gallery with me tomorrow, have a cuppa in the coffee shop and look around. There are all sorts of notices up about courses and workshops and things. Will you do that?

Nancy I'm just so tired, Nin.

Nina Well, it's late. We're all tired. Look at Max.

Max (*waking*) What's that? Nina, love, you're back. I must have nodded off.

Nina Very possibly.

Max Old age setting in. Nice time?

Nina Super. Really interesting.

Max Shall I whack the kettle on, you can tell us all about it?

Nina Actually, Max, if you don't mind, I'm absolutely shattered.

Max (*disappointedly*) Righto, no, that's fine. I'm quite tired myself really.

Nina I mean, you're very welcome to stay and pace around all right with Nancy. She does a fine line in nocturnal mad-woman-in-the-attic style wringing of hands, don't you, pet?

Nancy Because I have bad dreams.

Nina Well, we'd all have bad dreams if we went to bed on a full jar of pickled onions.

Max She hasn't had a single one tonight. Just cups of tea and a couple of custard creams.

Nancy (*almost to herself*) In one dream I've got to be a lollipop lady.

Nina (*yawning stagily*) I'm exhausted ...

Max I should get going. (*He makes no move*)

Nancy You can be a lollipop lady 'till you're sixty-five.

Nina Well, thank you, Max, dear. I really appreciate this. (*She stands up decisively*)

Max A pleasure, Nina. Any time. Anything.

Nina Nancy, have you thanked Max for sitting with you?

Nancy (*forlornly*) Only I don't want to be a lollipop lady at all.

Nina (*sharply*) Nancy!

Nancy Yes, love?

Nina Have you said thank you to Max?

Nancy Thank you, Max.

Max A pleasure, Nance.

Nina picks up Max's jacket from the chair and helps Max on with it. The pickled onion on the fork sits jauntily in his breast pocket. Nina notices. She leans forward as though to fondly touch Max's lapel, and in a swift movement holds the fork up in front of him. Max stares at it, dumbfounded

Nina Trying to run off with the silverware again, Max?

Nancy looks sheepish

Max (*swift but unconvincing*) Oh! That's right! Yes, um, I felt a bit peckish earlier while I was making the ... Suddenly, and I must have just accidentally... As you do. (*Beat*) Old age, you see. I can't even remember where I parked my car tonight.
Nina Well, go and look for it, there's a dear. (*She leads Max to the door*)
Max I meant what I said tonight, Nina. You look lovely.
Nina (*gently*) Go home, Max.
Max Good-night, then.
Nina 'Night.

Max exits

Nina shuts the door and returns to the room

Christ. What does that man expect from me?
Nancy He loves you.
Nina I'm aware of that, Nancy.
Nancy He's a nice man. He's kind.
Nina I know he's kind. He's very kind. But I'm not going to *marry* the man just because he took the rap for your pickled onion habit. (*Beat*) Oh, it's not that I don't appreciate everything he does for us. I do. But I just hate the thought that he's totting up all his kindnesses, and at some point he's going to present us, present *me* with some huge receipt for all the times he's put himself out; gone out of his way; done us a favour. And the debt will be so enormous, so unrepayable that I'll ... I don't know.
Nancy Max would be kind to you.
Nina I'm tired, Nance. Let's go to bed.

Nancy remains motionless

What?
Nancy I can't move.

Nina *What?*
Nancy I can't move.
Nina Oh, Christ. What do you mean, you can't move?
Nancy I'm too sad.
Nina To *move?*
Nancy Just — heavy.
Nina Oh, too heavy, well, yes.
Nancy No, I mean, *heavy.* Inside. (*Beat*) I can't see the future, Nin.
Nina Well, I'm not exactly a clairvoyant, love.
Nancy No, I mean — *a* future. I can't see a future. (*Beat*) I'm frightened, Nin.

A pause. Nina takes a deep breath

Nina Nancy, you lost your job. That's all. It's a bugger and a shame and it
    isn't fair, but it happened. It *happens.* And people cope. They adapt. They
    survive. And you weren't a miner, or a docker, you were a shorthand typist,
    and in five years you'd be retiring anyway. Now I know you've lost your
    routine, and you're a bit low, but it isn't the worst thing that could possibly
    happen. You're well and healthy and as long as I keep working, perfectly
    secure, and we live in a nice warm flat with plenty to eat, more than plenty
    in your case, and quite frankly, love, I don't think you've got all that much
    to complain about. I'm not being unsympathetic. But the way you're
    behaving, anyone would think — I mean, you're *grieving*, Nancy. You're
    mourning. (*Beat*) And no-one's died.

Black-out

SCENE 5

The National Gallery *café*

*Zelda and Philip sit at a café table. He is writing on a piece of paper. She
stares straight ahead, smoking. Her bag is beside her chair. There is a
noticeboard. The mood is fragile, although initially playful; there is a sense
that the end is nigh. Philip looks up suddenly*

Philip I don't know how to say this.
Zelda (*sharply*) Say what?
Philip This. The advert. I don't know what I'm asking for.
Zelda Oh, right. Put "Desperately seeking someone seriously unattractive,
    in the hope that I can keep my great big wandering hands off them". That
    should do it.
Philip (*writing*) Great — big — wandering — hands …
Zelda (*laughing*) OK, no. "Desperately seeking someone who looks like a

horse —".

Philip I've known some gorgeous horses. But they're bad at sitting still.

Zelda How about someone who looks like a man? Or hang on, why don't you ask for a real man? Supposing such a thing exists.

Philip (*smiling*) You're being immensely childish.

Zelda What would you like me to be?

A pause. Philip puts down his pen

Philip I'd like you to be happy.

Zelda Oh. But?

Philip But. But I can't make you happy, Zeld.

Zelda So you're going to stop trying? (*She looks at Philip*)

Philip looks down

Do me one favour, Philip. Just one thing.

Philip Of course. Anything.

Zelda Just, let *me* say it. Let me say the words.

Philip Oh, sweetheart —

Zelda And don't put the fucking advert up until I've left this room or I'll rip it straight down.

Philip stares at her a moment, then he laughs

What? What are you laughing at?

Philip Nothing, nothing. You just reminded me for a minute of a girl I ——

Zelda Fine, shut up, enough! Philip, I remind you of a million girls, I remind you of every other girl who's been blessed enough to guest-star in your epic episodic sodding life! And if I was as ancient as you are, you'd remind me of a hell of a lot of boys.

Philip I don't doubt that.

Zelda Meaning what?

Philip (*gently*) Just that you're a — special girl.

They look at each other

Zelda Oh, God, I'm jumping off your conveyor belt, Philip. I don't want to come rolling around again. Go and find some fresh blood, go and get yourself some little A-level princesses. Then you can tell them they remind you of a special girl called Zelda.

Philip No, no more women. That's the whole point.

Zelda Oh, Philip, bullshit.

Philip I mean it, I'm serious. I'm giving up.

Zelda For Lent?

Philip For life.

A pause. Zelda lights a cigarette

> *Nancy enters with a tray of tea. She seats herself nearby and starts pouring the tea. She looks around for sugar*

Zelda When I was thirteen, I gave up kale for Lent.
Philip Kale?
Zelda It's a kind of curly green vegetable, like cabbage. I'd never eaten it in my life.

Philip reaches out and strokes the side of Zelda's face. After a moment she moves her head away. Nancy, starting to lean over and borrow some sugar, subsides when Zelda speaks

> You know what I don't get? Why now? I mean, sure, we've had problems, but we were going to overcome them, weren't we? That was the plan, wasn't it? We were going to overcome them. We were going to be fine.
Philip But sweetheart, we weren't fine, were we? For a long time. (*Beat*) Zelda, I'm forty-eight. And someone sitting not too far from me now said it was high time I grew up and stopped ——
Zelda Fucking around. I said it was time you stopped fucking around.
Philip Exactly.

Zelda gives a sharp shocked laugh

> No, I mean—I'm just trying to get my act together. I'm just stepping back a bit, taking stock.
Zelda That's bullshit, Philip, that's trite meaningless crap. You're doing this because you got scared, because you had a drop too much to drink and smoked some of the pot you've kept in your sock drawer since 1965, and you had an intimation of mortality. And you looked around and saw your life, and your wasted talent and your shipwrecked grand career and your kids who don't speak to you and all your weeping women, and understandably it scared you that in forty-eight years you've managed to achieved precisely *fuck-all*!

A short pause. Philip smiles

Philip Nice speech.
Zelda Nothing I say could even graze you, could it?

Nancy seizes her moment and leans over

Nancy Excuse me.

Philip and Zelda look at Nancy

Um... Is there any sugar in there, at all?

Wordlessly, Zelda passes her a sachet of sugar

Ooh, um, actually — is there any *sweetener*, at all? Sweet 'n' Low or Canderel or something? (*Beat*) Sorry, I usually have some in my bag but ...

Irritated, Zelda passes her the whole bowl of sweetners

Thank you, love. Sorry.

Zelda turns back to Philip. Philip is writing on his piece of paper again

Zelda You can't even concentrate on me when you're leaving me.
Philip I've got to get this done, Zeld. (*He finishes what he is writing, takes the notice to the noticeboard and pins it up.*)

Zelda sits still, fighting back her tears. Philip returns to the table

(*Noticing Zelda's distress*) Darling ——
Zelda (*recoiling*) No, Philip, you don't understand! This is *anger*! I'm *angry*! But I cry. I can't help it. It's instinctive; it's ingrained. Little girls aren't supposed to get angry; anger's unfeminine; it's unflattering, it makes your face red. For boys, it's the other way round, isn't it? Stamp and shout and throw your weight around but never shed a tear. Women forget how to be angry. We have crying instead. The acceptable face of this fucking *rage*.
Philip Oh, Zelda. "Men and women", "boys and girls". Why does everything have to come down to sex?
Zelda *You're* asking *me* that? (*Beat*) Because everything does.

Philip wearily rubs his eyes and drags his hand across his jaw

(*She looks at Philip*) I hate it when men do that.
Philip What?
Zelda Rub their eyes like that. So wearily. My dad does it. Men always do it. Makes you look old and tired and disappointed. I hate it.

Philip Sorry.

Zelda rises and stalks over to the noticeboard. During the following dialogue, Nancy looks up sharply; more alert than we have seen her yet

Zelda (*reading the notice; scathing*) "Preferably middle-aged. Any shape or size will do". God, you're desperate. (*She returns to the table and picks up her bag. She looks down at Philip*) When I met you, I thought you had the saddest face I'd ever seen. The saddest eyes. And I thought I'd cheer you up. I thought I could. (*Beat*) It's taken me all this time to realize you never wanted to be cheered up at all. You *wanted* to be miserable. It suits you better. Goes with your starving artist image. Goes with your clothes. So be miserable, Philip, be fucking miserable. (*Beat*) You don't think I know anything about anything. Well, I know this. I'll be all right, in the end; I'll be fine. But you, Philip. (*Beat*) No-one's ever going to love you this much again, you sad old man.

Zelda exits, tearing down and crumpling the advert as she goes

A pause

Philip follows Zelda, calling her name

Nancy waits a moment, then tiptoes over to the crumpled paper. She picks it up, uncrumples it and begins to read

Black-out

SCENE 6

The art studio

The plinth is set C. There are artist's easels laid out DC. There is tape-recorder set beside the plinth. There is a supply-cupboard US and an old-fashioned portable heater and arc lamp in the corner of the studio. Philip's jacket hangs on a hook on the back wall of the studio

Luka, eighteen, a handsome, elfin boy sits at an easel. He is sharpening pencils into a wooden box. He continues this action throughout the scene

Josie enters. She is aged thirty-nine and is brittle and elegant in a Barbour jacket. She carries her handbag

Josie Hallo, Luka. Nice Easter?

Luka nods his head

Any sign of our illustrious professor?

Luka shakes his head

Pity. I wanted to catch him before anyone got here. Still. Probably not a bad thing. I'd only have made a fool of myself again. (*Beat*) What must you think of us all? But, you keep it to yourself. It's rare, that. Most of us talk all the bloody time. I know I do. It's the therapy, you see. The first time you go, you think, how can I possibly open my mouth and my heart to this stranger? How can I ever start to *speak*, let alone tell the truth? But then, when you do, it's surprisingly easy. And it becomes addictive. And then, if you do it for long enough, you start to do it with everyone. I do, anyway. Just open my mouth and "plop", my life falls out. I'm doing it now. (*Beat*) I like you, Luka. Is that saying too much again? I was brought up to believe that you shouldn't let people know how much you like them. Shouldn't appear too eager. Let them come to you. But I've never been able to quite pull it off, the cool disregard. I always feel like our dog, bounding up, all over-enthusiastic, trying to mate with people all the time. Not that *I* try to mate with people all the time. (*Beat*) Not all people, anyway.

Philip enters, looking distracted

Josie turns instantly skittish and kittenish

Philip We've got a paper crisis. Nothing to draw on and they've padlocked all the bloody supply cupboards. Welcome back.
Josie (*unconcerned*) Oh dear! Maybe we should draw on the walls in protest.
Philip Mm, it's a thought.
Josie Or on each other. Body art. Now that could be fun.
Philip (*dryly*) Or not, as the case may be.
Josie So, Philip. How's the lovely Zelda?
Philip Fine, thank you. How's Angus?
Josie Oh, you know. Rich.
Philip No sign of Sylvia, Luka? She's normally here before I am.

Luka shakes his head and shrugs

Josie Well, that's because her son has usually dropped her off on his way back from Downing Street or Buckingham Palace or the bloody Pentagon.
Philip Maybe he couldn't fit her in today.
Josie What, in his car?
Philip In his schedule. Don't be bitchy.
Josie I'm not being bitchy. I just sometimes can't help wondering whether Sylvia's son actually exists. (*Coy*) Am I horrible?
Philip I've seen him.

Josie Have you? And?

Philip And what?

Josie Well, what does he look like?

Philip I don't know. Medium height, mid-thirties; I don't know.

Josie Ah, but if Sylvia had a *daughter,* you'd be able to describe her in intricate detail.

Philip Probably.

Josie You're no fun to pick on, Philip, you're too guilty.

Philip I know.

Josie There you go again! Defend yourself, for God's sake! Unless you can't?

Philip We need some paper.

Philip exits

A pause

Josie D'you know, Luka, I read in the paper this morning that lemmings don't actually commit suicide. It's all a great big myth. I was so disappointed; all these years I've been waiting to join the lemming throng and leap off something into sweet oblivion. And now I find they're just into survival, like everyone else.

Bridget enters, early forties, woolly-jumpered and carrying a plastic bag

Bridget *Bonjour* all! Happy Easter! Martin's parking the car. All right, Luka? (*Beat*) How are you, Josie?

Josie Oh, fighting fit, thank you, Bridget. What's in the bag?

Bridget Cherry bakewells. I made too many. The boys were home at the weekend, so I did a bit of baking to go with the Easter eggs.

Josie Lovely. How old are they, your boys?

Bridget Well, Craig's twenty two, I can't believe it, twenty-two! And Gareth's eighteen, same as Luka here. You are eighteen, aren't you Luka?

Luka nods

Same as our youngest. You'd love Gareth; ever so comical.

Josie I can imagine.

Bridget What about your husband, Josie, has he got kids? You've never said.

Josie One, from his first marriage. A daughter, Fiona. She's in financial PR, lives in Fulham and is wonderfully open about her feelings for *me*.

Bridget That's nice. You never wanted kids of your own, then?

Josie I think the closest I get to feeling broody is when I see crocuses. All those little clutches of lilac and yellow, little screwed-up silk hankies in the grass. Then I feel almost unbearably tender. But then crocuses don't scream all night or shit themselves or get in the way when you're trying to slit your wrists.

Bridget laughs stagily, alarmed

Bridget Where has Martin got to, I wonder? I might just go and check if he's ...

Bridget exits, colliding with Philip in the doorway. Philip enters. He is preoccupied with still trying to break open the locked store cupboard

Josie Any luck?
Philip (*preoccupied*) Mm?
Josie Paper?
Philip Not enough. No sign of Sylvia?
Josie No, and I've scared off Bridget. Poor Martin's probably hiding in the car-park, crouched under his Lada. Why does she always say "I made too many", when she quite obviously bakes all this stuff especially for the class? Now I think of it, I'm not sure I believe in *her* sons either. I don't think Martin's capable of fathering *anything*.
Philip Josie ...
Josie He hates this class, you know. He only comes because she makes him.
Philip What's the matter with you today?
Josie It's cold. I've got chapped lips. (*Beat*) I miss you.

Philip glances warningly towards Luka

Philip Josie ...
Josie It's all right, isn't it, Luka? Luka knows.
Philip (*gently*) There's nothing to know, any more.

A frisson. Then Josie turns away sharply and rummages in her bag. She produces a compact mirror and reapplies her lipstick. Philip battles away at the supply cupboard

Sylvia, a stately lady in her sixties, enters

Josie (*brightly*) Sylvia, we were wondering about you.
Sylvia Good-evening, everyone. Sorry I'm a bit late, Philip. My son had to make a terribly urgent phone-call to the United States of America before he could bring me.

Philip Not to worry, Sylvia. We hadn't started yet.

Josie Was it the White House?

Sylvia I beg your pardon, dear?

Josie President Clinton, was it?

Sylvia Well, quite possibly, yes. What do I know, dear? I'm only his mother!

Josie (*soothing*) Of course you are.

Philip gives Josie a warning glance

> *Bridget enters, with her thin, tetchy husband Martin. He clearly has no desire to be there*

Bridget Look who I found!

Philip Excellent. Now, we've got a paper shortage. I've found some but not much. You've basically got two sheets each and you'll have to use both sides.

Martin It'll smudge. Be buggered up.

Philip Nothing wrong with a bit of smudging. Can be used to great effect. You can do me a sketch in the style of ... Daumier.

Sylvia Oh, I *loathe* Daumier! Horrible messy man.

Philip Well, then you shall have the spare sheet of paper, Sylvia.

Martin That's not fair.

Philip Well, tear it in half. Fight it out between you.

Martin We pay for these classes, you know. It was specified in the coursebook that paper would be provided.

Bridget Oh well! Never mind!

Martin Paper and drawing equipment, it said. Stubby pencils and broken charcoal, more like. I've got better drawing equipment in the back of my car.

Bridget Martin! Isn't your sketchpad in the car? It's full of spare pages, it's almost brand-new. We could use that!

Martin That's my *sketchpad*, though. For my *sketches*.

Bridget Ah, go on, pet, go and get it, there's a love. Just for today. There'll be paper provided next week, won't there, Philip?

Philip Reams of it. It'd be fantastic if you could lend us some for now, though, Martin. (*Beat*) Otherwise you've all had a bit of a wasted journey.

A moment of agonising choice for Martin between the lesser of the two evils. He becomes aware that all eyes are upon him

Martin (*with annoyance*) Oh — all right! Just a minute.

Martin exits

Bridget It's his Althora pad. That's why he's being funny about it. It's where he draws his maps.

Josie What's Althora?

Bridget He's in this group, they meet up, they come round to our house sometimes. They sit in the cellar; I don't know why. I tell them they can come and sit in the living-room but they say, "no", they like it down there. I take them some lemonade and biscuits and I leave them to it. He's been doing it for years.

Sylvia But what is it, dear?

Bridget Well, it's a kind of made-up land, called Althora. They've got it all worked out, all the details, the history and the geography and the environment and the inhabitants and everything. Martin does all the drawings. Hundreds of them. Maps and little hobbit creatures and graphs of the climate and things.

Sylvia How unusual.

Bridget (*an outburst*) Well, I hate it! Always hated it. It doesn't seem right to me, all those grown men sitting in the cellar in the dark, drawing maps of places that don't exist. (*Beat*) He doesn't do it so much now, though. We come here instead. I wanted us to have a hobby, something we could do together, once the kids had gone off to university. He didn't want to, at first, but he's warmed to it now. He enjoys it now, coming here. He loves it!

Martin enters. He slams the pad down in front of Philip

Martin Just don't bloody go using it all.

Philip starts tearing sheets of paper from the pad and handing them out. He gives several sheets to Luka

Nancy enters. She is dressed smartly. She hovers around the door, but no-one sees her

Philip All right, Luka, mate, we've got very limited supplies tonight, so try not to scrunch up everything you draw. Now, where's this wretched woman?

Nancy (*uncertainly*) Um — here.

Philip Oh, hallo. Is it Nancy?

Nancy (*faintly*) Um — yes.

Philip Great. Great. You found us all right?

Nancy Um, yes, I just got on a 43 bus, thank you.

Philip Smashing. OK, Well, meet the rest of our little group. This is Nancy, everyone. Nancy, this is Josie, Luka, Bridget ——

Bridget *Bonjour*, Nancy!

Philip Martin, and Sylvia.
Sylvia Hallo, dear.

Nancy murmurs a shy hallo. Philip puts a hand lightly on her arm

Philip Right, Nancy. Shall we make a start?
Nancy (*very nervously*) Yes — um, Philip, um, I just wondered, could I ask you something?
Philip Certainly, fire away. (*He escorts Nancy little way off from the others*)

Josie watches jealously

Josie (*generally*) Have you noticed how Philip develops an entirely different personality with new arrivals? Lord of the manor, all of a sudden. Welcome to my humble studio. Come and look at my etchings ——
Bridget Martin, show everyone all your maps and things!

Martin reluctantly opens his sketchpad and the others gather round. During the following, they others look with curiosity and murmur variations of "Ooh, look at that", "My goodness, what's that?", etc.

Nancy Um. Well — do I *look* all right?
Philip Look all right?
Nancy I mean, my clothes. I didn't know what to wear, you see. I didn't know how smart to be. I mean, when you see pictures in art galleries and things, the people always look ever so smart, don't they? So I didn't know. I've been in and out of that many outfits this evening!

Beat

Philip Er — Nancy, is this your first time? I mean, have you ever done this before?
Nancy Um, no, I haven't, actually. I'm actually a shorthand typist, by trade.
Philip Right. OK. OK. (*Beat*) I think I'd better explain something, Nancy. Ah — this is a life drawing class. We don't *wear* clothes in a life drawing class. Well, I mean, *we* do. You don't.

A stunned silence from Nancy. The others are still engaged by Martin's sketchpad. Josie keeps glancing over

Nancy You what?
Philip Surely you realized that! Life drawing — it's drawing from life. In the flesh, literally. We're studying the body, that's the whole point. It's not like portraiture.

Beat

Nancy Do you mean — no clothes *at all*?

Philip Well, I've got a little Chinese robe that you can slip on between poses, if you get chilly. But while you're up there, yes, we'd like to see you absolutely nude, please.

Nancy But ——

Josie (*calling*) I say, you two, you should see some of these creatures of Martin's. They're jolly good.

Martin That's not a creature, it's an Althora warrior. His hand, see, is like a Swiss Army Knife.

Josie Aren't you imaginative. Have a look, Philip.

They all look expectantly at Philip. Nancy is visibly panic-stricken but no-one seems to notice

Philip All right, Nancy? If you just pop through that door you'll find a little changing-room. Whip your togs off in there and bring any valuables back out with you. One of our other models had her engagement ring pinched from that room. It looks out onto the street and some bastard just stuck his hand through the window.

Josie Philip's just sore 'cause he gave her the ring in the first place.

Philip (*wearily*) Probably.

Josie He never fights back, you know, Nancy. You can say anything.

Nancy (*with a squeak*) Oh, yes?

Philip OK, Nancy, first door on the left, dressing room A, the star's room. Just for you.

Nancy stares in terror at the door. Everyone waits. Philip gently pushes her and she moves robotically past the assembled group

   Nancy looks back frantically as she exits

A moment

Martin She's a bit older than the usual birds.

Sylvia Well, those are just silly little girls, Martin. This is a real woman.

Josie The "usual birds", as you charmingly put it, look like boys with silicone implants. At least this one's got normal human hips.

Martin (*gloomily*) Bet she's all droopy, though.

Bridget Martin!

Philip Well, I wanted you to experience working with a different kind of skin-tone. Older flesh. You need to discover lines and wrinkles.

Sylvia Darling, I discover lines and wrinkles every morning.

Philip So do I, Sylvia, believe me. But this is a worthwhile exercise. You'll find that wrinkled middle-aged hide is a lot easier to draw than smooth firm young skin. There are no shadows on a young skin, you see, no hard bones, no sharp planes. Just soft outlines, just … (*He drifts off momentarily, then hastily resumes*) And as we know, drawing is all about light and shade. With older skin there are so many more tonal variations, tiny gradations, subtle textural shifts. You can really use the pencil or charcoal, really exploit your medium. You'll find it's a lot easier to draw Nancy than say, well, Zelda. For instance.

Sylvia I think she's awfully brave, at her age. I could never dream of it.

Martin Good.

Bridget Martin! (*Beat*) D'you think she's all right in there? She looked a bit nervous.

Philip I'll give her a shout. (*He goes to the door; calling*) Overture and beginners, please! Nancy, this is your call!

Nancy (*off; with a yelp*) Just a minute!

Philip She'll just be a minute.

A brief pause

Zelda appears in the doorway

Josie You know what I think?

Philip No, Josie. What do you think?

Josie I think our little Zelda has walked out on you. And *that's* why we suddenly need to experience a different kind of skin-tone. Am I warmish?

Philip No, Josie ——

Zelda (*theatrically*) Yes, Josie. Not that it's any of your business.

Philip Zelda. This is an unexpected ——

Zelda Just here to get my money, Philip. Hallo, everyone.

Philip Your money? I'm, er, a bit strapped for cash right now, Zelda.

Zelda A cheque will be absolutely fine.

Philip (*quietly*) Hey, look, why don't you pop over tomorrow? I'll have some cash by then.

Zelda Fuck off, Philip, write the cheque.

A shocked intake of breath comes from the group. Josie is enjoying herself hugely. A pause, then Philip goes to his jacket and finds a battered wallet. He takes out his cheque book

Philip What do I owe you?

Zelda You mean financially?

Josie laughs

Philip (*battling on*) We're talking what? Thirty quid?
Zelda Forty.

Pause

Philip Forty. (*He writes Zelda a cheque*)

Everyone watches Philip

> *Nancy enters, quietly. She is wearing the thin silk Chinese robe that Zelda wore in* SCENE 3. *She clutches it around her as she stands, shaking and sweating, by the door*

Zelda God, you do all stare, don't you? Even when I've got my clothes *on*.
Philip (*handing her the cheque*) There you go.
Zelda (*snatching the cheque*) Good. If this bounces, I'm going to get you under the Child Protection Act.
Philip Goodbye, Zelda.

Zelda turns on her heel and espies Nancy

Zelda What's this? Help The Aged?
Nancy (*weakly*) Hallo.
Philip Nancy has very kindly volunteered to replace you, Zelda.
Zelda You're kidding! Jesus, Philip, you *were* desperate! (*Beat*) Well, it's a lousy job, grandma. You freeze your tits off for two hours while this lot fuck about with their crayons, and they all completely ignore you. They don't even meet your eyes. You know why? (*Beat*) They're embarrassed. And they're a bit worried that nudity might be catching. They think if they say hallo to you their knickers might drop off. (*Beat*) Even when he gives you a break they ignore you. Even when you put your robe back on. No-one offers you a fag, no-one brings you a coffee and God forbid anyone should actually *thank* you for lying there like a fucking *Playboy* centrefold for the last half hour. (*Beat*) When you're posing they talk about you like you're deaf, like when you take your clothes off you lose the use of your ears. They get all fractious if you move a muscle by mistake, you can hear them *tutting* if you breathe too deeply. I got cramp once and one of them asked for his money back. (*Beat*) But you *get* cramp. You get pins-and-needles. And you get bored rigid. Which is of course, exactly how they want you. Nice and rigid. Like a *corpse*.
Philip Zelda, darling. Go home.

Zelda See? Total fucking objectification. 'Cause as far as they're concerned, you're just a load of squares and circles. They don't even draw your face. They just stare at you from the neck down and then they draw you and it looks like a fucking hippo. I look like a hippo so I shudder to think what you'll look like. And afterwards you go home on the bus thinking, God, am I that gross? Am I that grotesque? And then you think, hang on, look at *them*! I mean, look at them! (*Beat*) Life drawing? This lot can hardly draw *breath*.

Zelda exits, slamming the door

A moment

Philip I do hope that hasn't put you off, Nancy.
Nancy Um …
Philip Ignore Zelda, she's twenty. We'll treat you like a queen. Now, how much time have we lost? All right, Nancy, let's have you up here.
Nancy (*barely audible*) Um, Philip …
Philip Now, any position you fancy as long as it's comfortable. That's the main thing. A lot of the time we do quick five-minute poses, but I'm going to start you off with twenty-minutes, chuck you in at the deep end. So don't get yourself into any position that you might find hard to maintain.

Philip stands by the plinth, waiting for her. Nancy is frozen, gripping the robe

OK? So just whip the robe off, and we'll see how we get on.
Nancy Um, actually, Philip, um, do you mind if I — just for the first session do you mind if I keep … It's a bit cold in here … ?

Beat

Philip Is it? Right. Heater. Martin, can you drag it over? I don't like to use it for too long 'cause it's about a hundred years old but — here we go. This'll warm you up.

Martin drags the heater over with fairly bad grace. Philip plugs it in. Nancy now has no excuse. All eyes are upon her

Brilliant! We have lift-off!

In abject mortification, Nancy starts to pick at her belt

Wait!

A reprieve? Nancy halts, hope dawning on her face

No, sorry, Nancy, not you. Music. We always work to music. Help to build
up a mood. You carry on, make yourself comfy. Now, whose turn was it
to bring a tape?
Sylvia I believe it was mine, Philip.
Philip Great. What have you got?
Sylvia A very old favourite of mine. My son used to play it on the piano
before he was even ——
Josie (*softly*) Conceived?
Sylvia (*oblivious*) — classically trained.
Philip (*taking the tape*) Thank you, Sylvia.

Track 5.

*Philip takes the tape and puts it into the tape recorder. Nancy slowly, slowly
undoes the robe with trembling fingers. This is sheer agony for her. She is
desperately self-conscious, almost dazed. She simply can't believe what
she's doing*

A piece of very beautiful classical music begins to play

*Nancy inches her way on to the plinth. She sits at an impossibly awkward
angle, trying to conceal as much of herself as she can*

Philip (*with diplomacy*) Lovely. Great. Nice pose, Nancy. Um, if you could
just try to — *relax*, a bit more, if you can? You just look a wee bit — *tense*,
there. Good. Better. Just relax. (*Beat*) All right, gang, it's half-past, you've
got twenty minutes. And — action!

*The artists start to draw. They all have very distinctive styles: Bridget is
broad and sweeping, Martin is crunched up like a myopic schoolboy, Sylvia
does a lot of "artistic" squinting and measuring perspectives, making an
imaginary "frame" with her fingers, etc. Josie is slightly violent with the
charcoal, and Luka, puts pencil to paper, draws a line, frowns and crumples
up the page. He does this repeatedly until a small ocean of paper gathers at
his feet*

*As for Nancy, as the music rises, she is gradually overwhelmed by the
soothing, industrious mood. There is a sense of hypnotic serenity. Nancy's
muscles relax despite themselves, and she looks increasingly drowsy*

Philip paces between the easels, murmuring instructions

A spotlight comes up on one side of the stage

Nina enters into the spotlight. She is dressed as if for work. She speaks directly to the audience, in a cool, evenly-paced voice

Nina Both the composition and the pose are instantly reminiscent of the classical nude; the body outstretched, displayed, the weight resting on one elbow, and the head angled so that she might look out at us, and the observer might become the observed.

Philip Now remember, there are no straight lines in the human body. *Everything* curves. Hold your pencils loosely, get some sweeping lines, exploit that curvaceousness as much as you can.

Nina Note the rhythmic organization of the body, the repetition of shapes. The arcs and spheres that almost seem to symbolize the order and harmony of the universe.

Philip Gentle strokes, Josie, hold the charcoal further up. Lightly, that's it. She's not marble, she's marzipan!

Nina She is presented to us with all the studied artifice of the convention, yet stripped to her absolute essentials, her truest form.

Philip Just look at that elbow again.

Nina Begging the question: is she perfectly revealed, or is she perfectly concealed?

Philip I think we need a bit of chiaroschuro. Bit of light and shade. (*He goes to the corner and returns with an arc-lamp. He angles it towards Nancy*)

Nina Is indeed the naked body the most seamless and impervious disguise?

Philip All right. Let's shed some light on the matter. (*He switches on the arc-lamp*)

The lamp projects a strong, warm light over Nancy

Nina steps back into the shadows

A beat, then Nancy slowly turns her head towards the light

ACT II

Scene 1

The flat

A bright, summery light fills the room

Nina enters, rather hot and bothered. She picks up a letter from the mat

Nina Nancy? Nance? (*Beat; to herself*) Of course not. Silly me.

   Nina takes the letter into the kitchen to put the kettle on, and emerges, reading it

The doorbell rings. Nina hastily stuffs the letter into her pocket. She opens the door

   Max enters, carrying a toolbox and some planks of wood

   Max, dear. Bearing pine.
Max Your shelves, love, for the bathroom. You said tonight would be a good time to knock them up.
Nina Is it Wednesday already?
Max All day.
Nina Oh, well then. Mystery solved. *That's* where she is. Tea? Kettle's just boiled.
Max You're an angel. (*Referring to the planks of wood*) Shall I put these ...?
Nina Just lean them up against the wall. God, it's hot, isn't it?
Max And we thought summer wasn't coming!
Nina I can't stand it. Cooped up in that bloody mausoleum all day, wittering on about heritage to people who frankly would rather be out in Trafalgar Square videoing pigeons — I've had enough, Max, I really have. I'm sick of the sound of my own voice.
Max Sit down, love, you must be shattered: I'll make the tea.
Nina No, no, I'm fine. Honestly. You sit down. Be a guest.

   She goes into the kitchen

(*Off, raising her voice*) It's the journey, more than anything. The rush-hour's so awful. I'm going in on the Tube tomorrow, I don't care. I'm not spending another evening sitting at an angle half-way up the Archway Road, thank you. My shoulders are completely locked.

Max sits

After a moment, Nina returns with two cups of tea

Nina Sorry, I've no biscuits. She'll bring some, if she comes in. There's some woman in her class who seems to provide a constant supply of *pâtisserie*.

Max Her drawing class, is this?

Nina Well, apparently so, not that I've seen any actual drawings yet. It's extraordinary, you know Nance, she's never been in the least bit artistic, never shown any sign of *interest*, even, and then she joins this class and all of a sudden she's off at exhibitions half the time. I actually bumped into her in the Gallery the other day. I said, "What on earth are *you* doing here?" And she said, "Oh, just browsing." Browsing! Like she was wandering round hoping to pick up a bargain! Nice little Gainsborough or two!

Max Still. Sounds like she's happier.

Nina Oh, she's *happier*, all right. (*Beat*) I don't know, Max, I'm not sure I didn't prefer her depressed. I could certainly do without the singing.

Max Singing?

Nina All the time. It's driving me insane.

Max What does she sing?

Nina Oh, you know. Songs from the radio, jolly sort of 1950's showstoppers. Doesn't know the words, of course, it's all just la-la-la. I can hear her from the minute I wake up.

Max Nice and cheerful, though, to wake up to that.

Nina (*slamming down her cup*) It's infuriating, Max!

A pause. Nina picks up her cup again and sips

Max Are you sure you're all right, love?

Nina Yes. Yes. It's just this weather. It's too hot for me, I hate it. I'll be fine when it's bit cooler.

Nancy enters, carrying a plastic bag. She looks brighter and more summery than previously. She moves with a subtle but perceptible new confidence

Nancy Isn't it lovely out! You can't believe it! People are walking about like it's summer.

Nina Well, it *is* summer, Nancy.

Nancy But it's seven o'clock though, and bright sunshine, it's like abroad. They're all sitting outside that new pub with great big drinks. I thought, I could *murder* a lemonade shandy!

Nina Well, we're having tea. Bring yourself a cup in.

Nancy goes through to the kitchen, singing happily. She leaves the plastic bag in the living-room

Nina looks pointedly at Max, then goes over and peers into the plastic bag. She brings out a Tupperware container

Nancy returns with a cup

Don't tell me. What's-Her-Name made an excess of fairy-cakes again and brought them in for show-and-tell.

Nancy Bridget. They're caramel slices, they're ever so nice. Have one, Max.

Nina They look like concrete. I bet she uses wholemeal flour.

Nancy They're lovely though. I've had three. Two in the class and one when I was waiting for my bus.

Nina Well, you're a glutton. D'you want one, Max? Help yourself. (*She rounds on Nancy*) So. I don't suppose you brought any drawings home with you tonight?

Nancy I told you, love, I'm not good enough yet. Honestly. I'll bring something home when I've improved a bit. I've not done anything worth keeping yet.

Nina Well, it's all very annoying. I keep waiting to see some evidence, Max, that she's actually *doing* something in this class, and all she brings home are pieces of cake. I'm beginning to get highly suspicious about the whole thing. I think it's just an elaborate front for some sort of Tupperware party.

Nancy emits a nervous high-pitched laugh. They both look at her. A pause. Max senses that his presence is adding to the tension

Max Well, ladies. Lovely as your company is, I'd better get going with these shelves. You still want them on either side of the mirror, Nina?

Nina Please, Max.

Max Right then.

Max goes into the bathroom with his planks and his toolbox

A pause

Nancy (*nervously*) Um, actually, Nin, I've been wanting to mention something to you, just in passing.

Nina Since just passing seems to be what we do these days. Go on then, what is it?
Nancy Um. Well, it's about my art class.
Nina Yes?
Nancy Well, um, what it is, is — *in* the art class … Um …
Nina Oh Nancy, do spit it out, I want to start dinner.
Nancy (*rapidly*) Well, in the art class ——

Max begins to hammer thunderously *in the bathroom. Nancy is completely drowned out. They sit in silence whilst the noise goes on. Finally, it stops. Nina rises*

Nina Thank God for that. A two-minute reprieve while he carves my name in pine. Right. Dinner. (*She moves towards the kitchen. She stops at the door*) Sorry, Nance, were you saying something?

Nancy just looks at her helplessly

Black-out

Scene 2

The art studio

Nancy has just finished posing for all the group apart from Luka. She wears the Chinese silk robe. Philip is pacing

Martin That was never five minutes!
Philip According to my watch, old chap.
Martin I hadn't hardly started!
Philip Well, that's the nature of the exercise. You have to work fast.
Martin Fast? Speed of bleeding light, *"old chap."*
Bridget It was a bit tight, Philip. I only did her ear.
Philip You're not supposed to do her *ear* at all, Bridget! I just wanted you to get a very basic outline of her body, the form she creates. Why do you lot always have such trouble with this concept? (*He looks at Josie's sketch*) Josie. Try to see the negative shapes, if you can. See there, for instance, where the bent knee makes a triangle. Try to see the negative as a shape rather than a space.
Josie Gosh, and I'm usually so quick to see the negative! The Prozac must be kicking in at last. My husband will be delighted, I must e-mail him.
Bridget E-mail him?
Josie Yes, it's our primary mode of communication. The cosy intimacy of the worldwide web has done wonders for our marriage.

Bridget What does Angus actually *do*, Josie?

Josie (*airily*) Oh, shoots things, screws things, drinks little see-through drinks. Bullies smaller boys in cyberspace. I don't know. We don't meet all that often, Bridget, we keep rather different hours. When I wake up he's usually locked in the loo with his *Financial Times*, and by the time I'm actually *alive* he's out in the Docklands kneecapping young accountants.

Sylvia My son reads the *Financial Times*. He's obliged to, in his line of work. (*Beat*) I don't think he reads it in the lavatory, though.

Philip Could I have your attention for a moment, children? I'm trying to conduct a class here.

Josie When I first met Angus, I had a dress that was the precise colour of the *Financial Times*. Liked poached salmon, peach roses, pink champagne. I loved that dress. I used to wear it a lot in the early days, in the hope that he might — read *me*, instead. (*Beat*) I expect I've still got it somewhere. Gathering dust.

Philip A touching story, beautifully told. Now if we could turn our minds to life drawing, momentarily?

Bridget When I met Martin, I was dressed as a camel. It was fancy-dress. I was the front and my friend Wendy Bostick was the back. We were a dromedary.

Josie What was Martin?

Martin I wasn't anything.

Philip Back to the drawing-board, then.

Sylvia My late husband and I met at Crufts.

Philip Christ!

Sylvia My little Valentina won "Best Small Bitch".

Josie I should be up for that.

Philip Watch that line, Martin. Look at the length of her legs compared to her body.

Martin Yeah? What's wrong with them?

Philip Well, you've made her look a bit like one of your — creatures. What's that sort of, sting-ray thing, coming from her shoulder?

Martin It's her *arm*. And we don't have women in Althora.

Josie (*beat*) Philip can't contemplate a world without women, Martin, it's beyond him.

Philip (*grimly*) I'm trying, Josie. I'm trying.

Josie Do you have *schoolgirls* in Althora, Martin?

Philip wheels around as though about to hit her but turns on her drawing instead

Philip Being a bit heavy-handed there.

Josie Oops.

Philip (*looking at the drawing properly*) Nice torso, though.

Josie That's the most romantic thing you've said in weeks.

Philip Right, at this point, I give up. You can all go home, before Martin's drawing gets up off the page and annihilates us all. Go on, shoo, the lot of you. Nancy and I have work to do.

Josie Ah, the famous painting.

Josie witnesses the following little exchange with elevated eyebrows

Philip I'm just going to grab a coffee, Nancy. Want anything?

Nancy Ooh, cup of tea, please, Philip.

Philip (*remembering*) Milk, no sugar, you've got your sweeteners.

Nancy (*smiling*) That's right.

Philip exits

Josie Is it me, or is he remarkably keen to get rid of us today?

Bridget He's obsessed with his painting, bless him. Can't wait to get his hands mucky.

Josie That much we know. So when do we get to see this masterpiece, Nancy?

Nancy Oh, I'm not sure, to be honest. He says if it goes well we might have a little unveiling.

Josie Well, I'm never averse to a little unveiling. (*Beat*) You've got him well-trained.

Nancy How d'you mean?

Philip appears quietly in the doorway, holding two plastic cups

Josie Well, I bet he doesn't know how I take *my* tea. And I've *slept* with him.

Philip Coffee, isn't it?

Josie jumps. Bridget stifles a nervous giggle

Black, I believe. No sugar. (*Beat*) Now go away. (*Beat*) All of you!

They all trail sheepishly to the door

Hang on. Where's Luka today? Anyone know?

Nancy Um, yes. It's his test. For his motorbike. Driving test.

They all look at her

Josie How does *she* know?
Nancy Well — he told me?
Philip In *words*?
Nancy Um, no, not really.

An expectant pause

He showed me his crash-helmet. I ask a lot of questions. (*Beat*) He sometimes nods.
Philip Well, thanks for clearing that up for us, Nancy. Now everyone can be on their way.

Sylvia, Martin and Bridget exit

Josie hesitates

Can I help?
Josie No. It's just — no. Must dash.

Josie exits

Philip starts arranging his drawing-board, angled so that the painting is not visible to the audience. Nancy sits, sipping her tea

Nancy (*referring to the robe*) I'll take this off in a sec.
Philip It's all right, Nancy, I'm working on the face again today. We've reached a difficult point, actually. What I call the "second eye" moment.
Nancy What does it mean?
Philip It means, my dear, that I've successfully painted the left side of your face, up to and including your left eye. Now, the eyes are always the great challenge for me, so at this point, I panic. Because now, it's serious. What if the second eye isn't as good? Or goes wrong? Or seems to be looking in the other direction? If the first eye wasn't up to much, it wouldn't matter, I could always chuck the whole thing in and start again. But because I'm pleased with it, the stakes are raised. It could be, potentially, a damn good painting. In short, if I fuck it up now, I'm buggered. (*Beat*) Sorry, Nancy.
Nancy I don't mind having funny eyes.
Philip No, I mean my appalling language, sorry.
Nancy I'm not fussed about swearing. Nina swears all the time.
Philip Does she really?
Nancy Well, she mostly just says "Jesus Christ". I don't know if that counts as swearing, it's only His name. And she usually just says one bit at a time, like, "Christ, Nancy, are you going to *eat* that?". (*Beat*) She's ever so edgy at the moment, though. Fed up with her work, I think.

Philip Yes. Aren't we all.

A pause. Philip paints

Nancy Don't you like it then, teaching?

Philip (*wearily*) Oh, Nancy. Where to start. (*Beat*) Do you realize, this is the first painting, by myself, *for* myself, that I've attempted in just over five years? Well — correction. I have *attempted* others.

Nancy Did they go wrong then?

Philip Zelda calls it artist's block. This solid white wall that you can't get over, or under, or around. This paralysing doubt. This fear, not that you can't do it, but that you won't do it well. Or you won't do it as well as you *could* do it. So you don't do it at all.

Nancy (*warmly*) But you're doing it now.

He looks at her and smiles

Philip Yes, I — seem to be. Thanks to you.

Nancy Me? But I just sit here, love.

Philip That's all you need to do. (*Beat*) I can paint you because — I can *see* you. There's no clutter. It's simple, clear, organic. I'm here, you're there. (*Beat*) I thought if I cut off from all my — involvements, that I might be able to paint again. I've got two kids who are older than most of my involvements, and I'm not nearly involved enough with *them*. They send me these letters from places like Goa where they're teaching English and building schools, like we should all be doing. These long letters, always seem to be written on tissue paper. (*Beat*) Their mother, Anna, she's a fantastic woman, sometimes I wish I could just — but she's remarried, he restores furniture, they live in Taunton. (*Beat*) Then there's Josie. She's one hell of an involvement, poor Josie, with that lousy grouse-shooting husband of hers. For some reason she thinks I can help her, but I can't, Nancy, I can't help any of them. I can't be what they want from me. I can only be this. (*Beat*) This man, who isn't as good as he could be. Who *can't* be as good as he *is*.

Nancy What about that Zelda?

Philip (*sighing*) Ah, that Zelda. Have you ever done anything you've regretted, Nancy?

Nancy I've never done anything at all. (*Beat*) I regret *that*.

Philip Never too late, Nancy. (*He returns to his painting*)

Nancy stares at Philip wonderingly: this is an entirely new idea to her

Nancy (*softly*) Isn't it?

Philip Could you just — lift your chin a fraction? That's it.

A pause

Nancy (*suddenly*) She doesn't know I'm here. Nina, I mean. (*Beat*) I mean, she knows I come here, but she doesn't know what I do. She thinks I'm learning to draw.
Philip Crikey. Can you not tell her?
Nancy Oh, Philip, I should have told her months ago!
Philip Why didn't you?
Nancy I did mean to. I still do. I sit here, every week, and I go through the conversation in my head. How I'll say it. What words I'll use. Will I tell her before dinner, or during, or after, when we're washing the pots? Or will I maybe let her watch the News first, the Nine O'Clock News, we usually watch. Sometimes I think, and this really is terrible, I think that if I told her after the News, and something really shocking had happened, like a plane crash or a war, then she might not be that angry with me. It might not seem that awful, by comparison. That's a dreadful thing to think, isn't it? I know. (*Beat*) I've tried to tell her, once or twice. But every time I open my mouth to say it I seem to just — close it again. Or say something daft instead. And now it's too late, now I've passed the point where it might have been all right. 'Cause now I'm a liar as well.
Philip As well as *what*?
Nancy Well, as well as a — (*mouthing*) *nude model.*
Philip But for heavens' sake, Nancy, modelling for a life class is hardly a federal offence, is it?
Nancy You don't know Nina.
Philip I'm beginning to feel rather glad about that.

During the following, unnoticed by either Philip or Nancy, Josie returns to the studio

Nancy She's always been angry. Always. Even when she was a little girl. Even when she was a tiny baby, when they first brought her in from the hospital. She'd lie there and look at you with this little frown, and with her mouth all pinched, like you'd got on her nerves. It's treading on eggshells round our Nina, always has been. (*Beat*) When she was in her twenties, she went off to Italy for a year, to Florence, to do her Art History. And when she got back, she was different. Sort of like, she'd decided something. Still angry, but a different kind of anger. (*Beat*) Angrier, in a way.

Josie steps forward

Josie Philip.

Philip looks up, surprised

Philip Josie.
Josie Sorry to interrupt.

A beat

Philip Well, that's all right. What can we do for you?

Josie bursts into tears

Oh, dear God, Josie, *what*? Tell me, what?
Josie (*sobbing*) Five minutes, Philip! Five short minutes of your precious
time! Is that too much to ask, when you've ——
Philip Josie, I'm in the middle of ...

Josie's sobbing threatens to rise

All right. Come on. Let's get you a cup of tea or something. Coffee. Black.
No sugar. (*He moves to Josie and turns her gently towards the door*) Sorry,
Nancy, I'll be exactly five minutes, won't I, Josie? You can time me.
(*Referring to the painting*) And no peeking.
Nancy Who, me?
Philip (*holding up five fingers*) Time me.

Philip and Josie exit

*Nancy sits a moment, and then rises. She moves cautiously towards the
painting*

Without Nancy noticing, Zelda appears at the door

Just as Nancy is about to reach the painting, she hears Zelda

Zelda No peeking, he said.
Nancy Oh!
Zelda Don't worry, I won't tell.
Nancy Where did you spring from, Zelda?
Zelda I was waiting round the corner. I was going to come in but then he
stood up and I — didn't intend to, but I found myself kind of — hiding.
Silly. It's been four months. I thought I was ready. (*She laughs*) Heart's
banging.
Nancy He'll only be five minutes.

Zelda With that fruitcake? Half an hour, at least. She won't even have got
his trousers off, let alone told him her problems. (*She moves further into
the room and looks at the painting*) This is good. Really good. You've
broken his block. (*Beat*) When he used to say, "I can't paint properly until
I've made love to the model", I used to wonder how he dealt with still lifes.
You know, bowls of fruit. Antlers.

Nancy (*beat*) How d'you mean?

Zelda What?

Nancy In what way?

Zelda stares at her

Zelda Do you mean, you haven't?

Nancy Haven't what?

Zelda My God, don't tell me you're the exception!

Nancy To what?

Zelda Nancy, you've been coming here since I left. That's four months.

Nancy (*mystified*) You've lost me, love.

Zelda Four months. With Philip. And you haven't had sex.

Nancy *Sex?*

Zelda Is it something you've heard of?

Nancy With *Philip*?

Zelda All right, he's not that bad!

Nancy Zelda, bless your heart, I'm a good seven years older than him!

Zelda He's not fussy.

Nancy But child, look at me! Do I look like the kind of woman who ——

Zelda Philip doesn't have "kinds" of women. He just has women.

Nancy (*decisively*) Well dear, he's not had me.

A pause

Zelda Sorry, I just — leapt in there. Making assumptions. (*Beat*) You must
think I'm incredibly rude.

Nancy 'Course not, love. (*She takes a packet of Polo mints from her robe
holds out the packet*) Polo mint?

Zelda No, thanks. What I really want is a cigarette. I've given up.

Nancy Good girl.

Zelda Gave up fags and Philip in the same week. Philip was actually easier.
(*Beat*) I've been so jealous of you.

Nancy Of *me*?

Zelda I couldn't help him, you see. I think because I wanted to, too much.
It mattered too much. And maybe for the wrong reasons. Maybe I wanted
it for me, not for him. Wanted to be his muse, his inspiration, to reignite
whatever it was in him that had – gone out. And I suppose I'd rather banked
on being irreplaceable.

Nancy But Zelda, there's no comparison! I mean, I'm not anyone's *muse*! Look at me, for heaven's sake! I just sit here like a big bag of marshmallows!

Zelda Then why can he paint you, when he couldn't paint me?

Nancy Well, it's simple, love. Same as he can paint a bowl of fruit.

A pause. Zelda absorbs this

You're a beautiful girl, Zelda. You're young, you've your whole life ahead of you. Philip's just — one man.

Zelda Funny, though. Men like Philip, they're never alone for long. There's always a Josie waiting in the wings with a dustpan and brush.

Nancy Ah, you'll meet someone else, someone your own age. You're a young woman. You should be having fun, having a bit of romance, not fretting yourself silly over a big soft man like him.

Zelda Being a young woman isn't like a Tampax ad, you know. We're not all paragliding and rollerblading and jumping for joy 'cause we're wearing pantyliners or drinking Coke or even bloody snorting it! Most of us are just trying to work out who the fuck we are.

Nancy Well, I'm fifty-five and I still don't know. And I didn't even know I didn't know, 'till recently.

Zelda It's you lot that screw us up, though. Telling us that these are the best years of our lives. Telling us we're at our peak and in our prime when we're mostly bloody petrified! Scared, all the time. Scared of sex, scared of AIDS, scared of getting pregnant. Scared of growing up. Scared of *not* growing up. (*Beat*) I've been seeing this bloke, actually. Don't tell Philip.

Nancy Of your own age?

Zelda Couple of months younger, in fact.

Nancy Is he a nice lad?

Zelda He's sweet. We have fun together. Do things young people are meant to do. Go clubbing, go drinking, take too many drugs. Have sex in silly places, at silly angles. It's fun. (*Beat*) Thing is, though, sometimes, I don't feel like it. Any of it. I'm in some dark club and the music's pounding and I'm waiting for some track I could possibly dance to, or I'm waiting to be pissed enough to want to dance at all, and I'm wishing for it to stop, just to stop so I can hear myself think — and I just want to be at home in my pyjamas eating Marmite off a spoon.

Nancy I don't blame you, from the sound of it.

Zelda Sometimes I look at Dan, this boy I'm seeing, and I just wish we were *old*. I wish we'd done all this, and we were out the other side, and safe, and it was all behind us. Just stuff to tell the grandchildren. No more perils, no more thrills, no more highs and lows. Just a sort of gentle drifting. Relinquishing all this shit.

A pause

Will you tell him I was here, Nancy?

Nancy He'll be back any minute.

Zelda I know, but I'm not quite ready, yet. (*Beat*) Will you tell him I'm going
away, travelling. I'm going backpacking round Europe. And I'd like to see
him before I go, just for a drink, just to say goodbye. Case I get devoured
by rabid youth-hostellers or something. Will you tell him?

Nancy Are you going with — Dan?

Zelda No, I'm going on my own.

Nancy My goodness, aren't you brave!

Zelda Well — nearly, yes. I will be. (*Beat*) Actually, I think I'd like one of
your Polo mints, now, if that's all right. For the journey. Keep me going.
Is that all right?

They smile at each other

Black-out

SCENE 3

The flat

*Nina emerges from the kitchen, highly agitated. She holds a jar of pickled
onions. She paces, eating them very fast*

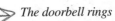 *The doorbell rings*

*She quickly takes the onions into the kitchen and returns, wiping her mouth.
She opens the door to admit Max*

Max (*concerned*) Nina, love —

Nina Come in, Max. Thanks for getting here so quickly.

Max What's all this about, then? You sounded ——

Nina (*sharply*) Tea?

Max Er, yes, tea. Why not. Then we can sit down and you can tell me
what ——

Nina I'll put the kettle on.

Nina exits to the kitchen

*Max wanders round anxiously. He sits on the sofa, drumming his hands on
his knees*

Nina returns

Max stands up

Oh Max, we've known each other sixteen years, you don't have to stand up every time I walk into the room.

Max No. Sorry.

Nina Well, sit down, then.

Max (*sitting*) Nina ——

Nina (*erupting*) I mean, where is she, Max? Where the hell is she? She comes in, she goes out, devil-may-care, humming her little heart out — I mean, where does she *go*, for Christ's sake? What is she *doing*?

Max You mean Nancy.

Nina Well of course Nancy, who else?

Max She's doing her art class, isn't she?

Nina Two nights a week! Monday and Wednesday! Seven 'till nine! So where is she the rest of the time, pray tell? 'Cause she sure as hell isn't there! (*Beat*) And when she is, she might as well not be. Drifting round in a dream, in a daze. Humming. Grinning all the time like a Cheshire cat. She's — different, Max, and it's peculiar. If I didn't know better I'd think she'd taken a secret lover! A toyboy with a knack for home-baking.

Max Can you be sure she hasn't?

Nina Oh, come on, Max.

Max Stranger things have happened.

Nina Like what? (*Beat*) Tea.

She rises and heads for the kitchen. Max leaps up, struck by an idea

Max Hey, Nina. Tell you what.

Nina What?

Max Forget the tea. I've a bottle of red in the car. Jacob's Creek. What d'you say I nip out and get it? I'm only parked on the corner.

Nina It's three in the afternoon, Max.

Max So? There's no law says you can't have a glass of wine of a summer's afternoon, is there? They do on the Continent. I bet you spilled the odd drop in Florence.

Nina (*weakening*) Well, I don't know if ——

Max Come on, Nina! Do you good! Relax you, calm you down a bit. Put things in perspective.

Nina (*tightly*) Things aren't *out* of perspective, Max. But all right, if that's what you want, you may as well go and get it. I'd have been perfectly happy with Earl Grey.

Max Atta girl! I'll be two ticks.

Max exits. Nina goes into the kitchen, returns with the jar of pickled onions. She eats them furiously

Max is heard whistling

Nina ducks back into the kitchen as Max appears with two bottles of red wine. He heads for the kitchen just as Nina emerges: they all but collide in the doorway

Nina Two, Max?
Max Well. Just going to get a … (*He mimes a corkscrew*)
Nina Second drawer down on the left-hand side, mixed up with the chopsticks and all the other things we never use.
Max Second on the left.

Max goes into the kitchen

Nina returns to the sofa and sits

After a moment, Max returns with a tray, holding a bottle and two glasses

Madam requested the house red?
Nina Just the smallest drop for me, Max.

Max pours her a full glass. She recoils in horror

No, honestly, Max. Half of that. I mean it.
Max All right, just kidding. That can be mine.

He pours her a small glass. She accepts it distractedly

Cheers. Here's to us, hey? (*Beat*) Nina?
Nina Mm?
Max A toast. To — old friends.
Nina Old friends. Right.

They clink glasses

Max Been a long time, hasn't it?
Nina You were here yesterday.
Max No, I mean, since we all met. You and Nance, me and Pam. Sixteen years. (*Beat*) Long time.
Nina Mm. D'you ever hear from her, Max?
Max Who? Oh, Pam? Christmas cards. We used to do birthdays but one year I forgot and she never forgave me. But she's always been very zealous about Christmas cards.

Nina I remember. In fact, I think we still get one. Handcrafted from potato-
peel by pygmies, that sort of thing.

Max (*laughing*) That's about the gist of it. Well, she always liked you, you
and Nance.

Nina She thought you spent too much time here.

Max Yes, she found it — strange. (*Beat*) Said I was in love with you.

Nina (*laughing*) What, both of us?

Max No. Not both of you.

Beat

Nina More wine?

Max Nina——

Nina Max. Don't. Please.

Max Nina, I want to be here all the time.

Nina You *are* here all the time!

Max But I mean, not just — fixing things.

Nina Don't ask this of me. Please.

Max (*earnestly*) But why not, Nina? I mean ——

Nina Because the answer will always be no.

*Pause. She stands and moves restlessly about. Max sits still a moment, then
refills both glasses. He drinks his very fast*

Max Nina — I'd know, wouldn't I, if there was — anyone else?

Nina Oh Max, darling, I'm fifty-three!

Max And I'd have known, if there was.

Nina drinks. Then puts down her glass

Nina Well, all right. There was.

Max What?

Nina We're talking about a very long time ago. Thirty years, at least.

Max But — who?

Nina In Florence. Oh, don't look like a bloodhound, Max, it was decades ago.
I was twenty-three, for heaven's sake.

Max What happened, then?

Nina (*with difficulty*) Just — met this fellow. Englishman, living out there.
An art critic, journalist. Kept colliding for a while, you know, you spend
a lot of time in galleries, exhibitions, you start to recognize the faces.
Exchange a few words. And, eventually, spent a hazy afternoon amongst
some rather second-rate Tintorettos, and found myself, suddenly, involved.
Suddenly.

Max When you say "involved" … ?

Nina drifts away from him, in a world of her own

Nina And — *wanting* — something, with such certainty, and such conviction, came as quite a shock to me. Yes, I astonished myself. Behaved in a way that was quite — out of character. Became a different person. Suddenly.

Max Let me get this straight. You and this journalist chap, you had a — love affair, sort of thing?

She turns to look at him, focussing

Nina Yes. That's exactly what we had.

Max For what, a year?

Nina Eleven months.

Max Eleven months. (*Delicately*) And this was *thirty years* ago?

Nina Yes, but ——

Max But we're talking about a hell of a long time, Nina love! Thirty years is a hell of a long time! I'm not saying it wasn't a big deal for you, but isn't time supposed to heal all wounds, etcetera …

Nina But it doesn't, does it! It doesn't heal any wounds at all! Look at me! Look at you! Time might be a cracking *anaesthetist*, Max, but a great healer it ain't! *Nothing heals. Nothing.* We just learn to live with what hurts.

A long pause. Max looks at his hands

(*Briskly*) Anyway. It was my own fault, of course. I was too happy, that year.

Max How can you be *too happy*?

Nina Yes, too happy for my own good. And I knew it, that's the stupid thing, I knew it and I just kept on. It's insane, to let yourself be that happy. You have to keep a check on yourself, maintain some kind of control. Otherwise it's suicide. Because once you've been there, Max, once you've had that, everything else can only disappoint. (*Beat*) I sat on the plane home, and knew perfectly clearly that the rest of my life would be just — getting by. Getting through. With gritted teeth and a hardness inside. Not giving up, by any means, but settling for something. And accepting, yes, that was that. (*Beat*) So there we have it. That's that.

Max (*halting*) And I don't suppose you could see yourself – settling for me?

Nina Look. With the best will in the world, Max, you don't love me. You just love thinking you do. (*Beat*) I mean, you're not *in love* with me. And I think we're both a bit long-in-the-tooth for all that anyway, don't you? (*Beat*) You're just lonely, Max.

Max Everyone's lonely. That's not the point.

A pause. An impasse. Nina pulls the letter from SCENE 1 *from her pocket*

Nina (*almost shyly*) I've been offered a job. I had an interview last month and
   I've had an offer. To lecture part-time at Trinity College. European
   Painting and Sculpture, Giotto to Cezanne. I didn't say anything because
   I wanted to wait and see what happened, but now ——
Max Trinity College, Cambridge?
Nina Trinity College, Dublin. (*Beat*) It's supposed to be one of the top places
   for Art History now, but then they all say that.
Max Dublin?
Nina I haven't told Nance yet. Haven't had a chance.
Max You'd live in Dublin?
Nina Well why not, for heaven's sake?
Max But you've, you've lived in London all your life, Nina!
Nina (*tartly*) Apart from my year in Florence.
Max But Nina …

   Nancy enters, breezily

Nancy Hallo love, hallo Max! Sorry, I'm running ever so late. Let me just ——

   Nancy passes straight through to her room

Nina (*hissing*) Where's she *going*? Where's she *been*?
Max Dublin, probably. Seems to be all the rage.

   Nancy re-enters, hastily pulling on a jacket

Nancy I won't be late, I shouldn't think, Nin. See you later. Ta-ra!

   Nancy exits

Nina (*spitting with fury*) If she could just have the decency to tell me where
   the bloody hell she thinks she's going! Christ, it's like dealing with a
   teenager!
Max I don't understand why it's upsetting you so much, though. She's just
   finding her feet again, isn't she? I mean, I thought you *wanted* her to ——
Nina All I want, Max, is to know what *my* sister is doing with this mysterious
   new life she's acquired. So please tell me, what's so wrong with that, hey?
   What's not to know about that?
Max (*slowly*) Maybe — you don't really want her to be happy and busy and
   all that. Maybe you *want* her to be miserable and depressed and eating
   lumps of things, because that makes you the one who's all right. (*Beat*)

Maybe you need Nance to be sitting about moping, so's you can't sit hankering after old Michelangelo in Florence thirty years ago! Maybe you need her to be weak, to keep you strong!

A slight, dangerous pause

Nina Well, thanks for that, Max. It's a great help.
Max I mean, if it bothers you that much, why don't you go after her? She won't have got far, you can stalk her at a distance in the car.
Nina What?
Max If it bothers you that much. (*Beat*) Oh, what the hell. Shall we open the other bottle, love? Old time's sake?

But Nina is on her feet, looking for her keys

Nina?
Nina Sorry, Max, I think I might just …(*She moves to the door*)
Max Where are you going? You're not going to … ? You shouldn't be driving, Nina …
Nina Look, I won't be long. Will you be a love and check out that waste disposal for us? It's still not going down. Thanks, Max, you're a treasure.

Nina exits

Max stands up, then sits. He is lost in thought

Black-out

Scene 4

The art studio

The plinth has been pushed back and Philip's easel has been pulled into the centre of the room. His painting stands on it, covered with a cloth

Josie, Sylvia, Bridget, Martin, Luka and Nancy are all assembled around the easel. Luka carries a crash helmet. Philip stands beside his painting

Philip You've a long shelf-life, as an artist. Unless you get arthritis in your hands or cataracts in your eyes, there's no real reason to ever stop. Monet painted well into his nineties, and he was effectively blind. (*Beat*) But sometimes, you lose the desire. You lose the need. You stop seeing life with a frame round it. You stop thinking in colours. And when that happens, you need something, a catalyst, something to actually *want* it back. For me, that catalyst was a certain lady, and I think we all know who I mean.

Josie is visibly holding her breath

Philip I want to dedicate this painting to a truly super model, for her patience, and her kindness, and the grace she doesn't even know she has.

It's Nancy's moment. She is bright pink, beaming, the happiest she's ever been

During the following, Nina appears unseen in the doorway

Josie (*acerbically*) Come on then, let's see it.
Philip Here we go.

Philip pulls the cover off the easel. Nina takes a step forward

Nina *Jesus Christ.*

They all look at her. Nancy is rooted to the spot

Philip You must be Nina.

Nina advances slowly towards the painting

Martin And who's Nina when she's at home?
Philip Nina is Nancy's sister.
Bridget (*to Martin*) Nancy's sister. Shush.
Sylvia (*to Nina*) Nancy's sister! You must be awfully proud!
Nina I'm — lost for words, really.
Nancy Nin —
Nina Are there others? Or is this it?
Nancy Um, no. There are lots of others.
Sylvia We've all drawn her!
Nina I see. So you are, the regular model, for this art class, Nancy?
Nancy Um, yes.
Nina As opposed to being a member of the group.
Philip Look, is it really such a big deal?

Nina regards him as though he were an insect

Nina Who's he?

Nancy This is Philip, Nin, he teaches the class and he painted the ——

Nina (*to Philip*) All right, Philip, let's see if I can explain something to you. This woman in your not uncommendable painting here, is my sister. My pathologically shy and self-conscious sister. My sister with the hot flushes who never gets undressed in front of anyone, who has to take clothes back to shops all the time because she won't try anything on in the changing-room. My sister who wears a *girdle* in 1999 and a long-sleeved vest in August, and locks herself in the bathroom to get dressed! I don't think I've seen her naked since I was about *six*. I think the last time I saw her naked was on the beach at Bridlington with her face in a strawberry cornet! (*Turning on Nancy*) Remember that time when the window-cleaner saw you getting out the shower? You were completely hysterical! Remember when you opened the door to Max and you were expecting me? You were head-to-foot in a huge green towelling bathrobe and you still got in a state 'cause you'd nothing on underneath! "What if he saw something?", you kept saying! I mean, *think*, Nancy! Try to understand why this is a little surprising to me!

Nancy (*simply*) I'm good at it. Philip says I'm good at it.

Nina How can you be *good* at being naked?

Philip There's more to it than that, it's about stillness and poise — I thought you were an art historian?

Nancy (*quickly*) You have to sit in the same position for ever so long at a time, Nin, it's really hard to stay still —

Nina Nancy, you've spent fifty-five *years* sitting in the same position! Only normally you're wearing half of British Home Stores. (*Beat*) What you've done, that doesn't take any skill. It just takes mindless exhibitionism. You might as well become a stripper! If you're so bizarrely keen to sell your body!

Nancy I haven't sold my body. If anything, I've — bought it back. (*Beat*) And it isn't mindless. You do a lot of thinking, lying there, all that time. And not just here. Last few months, I've been wandering all round town. Just — looking at things. People. Just seeing it all. Sitting in cafés, with Luka here, or just on my own.

Josie With *Luka*?

Nancy Going to art exhibitions. I saw the Pre-Raphaelites at the Tate. I saw the Gauguin. I even went to the cinema on my own. Have you ever been to the cinema on your own, Nin? It's nice. You think, I can't go in there on my own, I should be with someone. But you can. You just sit there, in the dark, with your Pick-'n'-Mix all to yourself, and you watch the film. No-one bothers you. No-one pinches all your round Liquorice Allsorts. You just watch the film. And then you come out into the light and all the people are rushing about, doing their lives, and it's like you've been in another world. And you walk down the street and you just look. You just listen. And you can hear your thoughts. (*Beat*) I've probably done more thinking, last few months, than all the rest of my life put together. And I've been wondering, Nin. Why has nothing ever happened to us?

Nina Don't be silly, Nancy.

Nancy But don't you ever wonder? Aren't you curious?

Nina I don't know what you're talking about, Nancy. Of course things have happened to us.

Nancy Like what? (*Beat*) Things happen to people. Lives happen. People have stories. What do we have? I mean, we've had all the bits, all the details, all the odds and ends. But we haven't had *stories*. We haven't had *happenings*. Nothing's *happened*.

A pause

Nina I spent a year in a foreign country. I'd call that a happening.

Pause

Philip I think, Nina, that Nancy's trying to say ——

Nina (*whirling on him*) I'm well aware of what my sister's trying to say, thank you. Not just in words, but with this whole absurd gesture. And now that she's said it, I think she should go outside and get in the car, and we should go home, and say whatever is left to be said in the privacy of our own flat. Come on, Nancy.

Nancy (*slowly*) No.

Nina What?

Nancy I said no. I'm not coming.

Nina I see. How do you propose to get home, then? Sitting naked on the 43? Or were you planning a trip to the cinema this evening? Or perhaps a casual meander round the red light district?

Luka I'll take her home.

Martin Steady on!

Josie He spoke! Luka spoke!

Bridget Luka, love!

Sylvia What did he say?

Luka I said, I'll take you home, Nancy. (*He raises his crash helmet*) As long as you don't mind ... ?

The slightest hesitation, then

Nancy That would be lovely, dear. Thank you.

They all look at Nina

Nina Right. Well, I don't want to stand here feeling like the Wicked Witch of the West for much longer, so I'll see you later, Nancy.

Nancy Nin, wait. (*Beat*) I'm sorry I lied to you, love. I'm sorry I didn't tell you what I've been doing, all these months. But I'm not sorry I did it. I'm glad. (*Stronger*) 'Cause this is my happening, Nin. I came here. I did this. And even if I never come back again after today, it did happen. No matter what, it happened. It happened to *me*.

A pause. Nancy is trembling, defiant. Nina looks suddenly very weary

Nina Oh, Nancy. What do you want me to say, love? It's good, that you've found something. If this is what you want. It's good that you're being appreciated by these people, and you're — part of something. And if all this has given you some sense of self then — well, then that's good, too. (*Hard*) But in the end. In the end, Nancy, it has to come from *you*. From inside. Not from this lot. Not from their eyes on you. Because you're the one who'll have to sustain it when the lights go out and they walk away. Because they will walk away, Nancy. Because people do. And in the end, you're on your own. (*Beat*) I'll see you later.

Nina exits

Nancy takes an instinctive step after Nina, then stops. She comes back to the centre of the group. The class gather around her

Black-out

SCENE 5

The National Gallery Café

Philip and Zelda sit side by side. She has a huge rucksack by her chair. He is fiddling with a pencil. There is a crossword uncompleted on the table

Philip So when d'you go?

Zelda Saturday. Some ungodly hour.

Philip Excited?

Zelda I can't wait. I've been carrying this thing — (*she indicates the rucksack*) around with me all week. Practising. Only there's nothing in it apart from a copy of Cosmo and a flapjack.

Philip Where will you start?

Zelda Amsterdam. Then Copenhagen, Prague, Vienna, Venice, Rome and home through Paris.

Philip Now, when you're in Venice, what you must do is see the permanent
Dali exhibition. It's an absolute revelation, Zelda, I mean, watercolours
and etchings you'll never see anywhere else. (*Beat*) But I don't suppose
I'm allowed to boss you about like that anymore.

Zelda Don't be silly, Philip. I'd love to see the Dali.

Beat

Philip Good.

A pause

Zelda (*conversationally*) The other day, I was in this changing-room,
somewhere awful like Top Shop, and there was this girl. This beautiful girl,
like a ballerina. And she was standing in front of this full-length mirror,
completely naked, watching herself cry. Just, silently. These great big
peardrop tears rolling down her face. She didn't even look upset. She just
looked fascinated. Absorbed. Like she was watching some fantastic
foreign film. (*Beat*) Sometimes I see things, and I want to tell you.

Philip We used to watch fantastic foreign films.

Zelda They weren't all fantastic.

Philip No. Probably not.

Pause

Zelda Philip ... these last few months, could you feel it?

Philip Could I feel ... ?

Zelda Me. Disentangling. (*Beat*) I was all wound up in you, like honeysuckle.
And I've been trying, very carefully, to disentangle. To disengage. It's
taken ages, and it wasn't painless, but I think, I've finally done it. And I
wondered. Could you feel me letting go?

Philip I think — I know what you mean.

Zelda And we're both free, now.

Philip I don't know. (*Beat*) I don't know if I've entirely disentangled myself
from *you*.

Zelda Philip ——

Philip No, listen. I've been surprised by — the lack of you. Your absence.
It's as real as your presence. A shape, not a space. It fills the room.

Zelda (*gently*) Are you trying to tell me you miss me?

Philip Zelda, I could draw you with my eyes closed.

Zelda No, darling you couldn't draw me at all! You had a *block*, you couldn't
draw anything! It's only now, 'cause we're both free, and separate ...

Philip I could draw you now. With my eyes closed.

Pause

Zelda Nothing frightens me anymore. I used to be so scared, of so many
   things. Now I feel fearless. That's because of you, Philip.
Philip I just wish I could say the same.
Zelda You? What frightens you?
Philip Oh, lots of things. New Labour. Alzheimer's disease. Moths. (*Beat*)
   Most of all, I think, that you'll forget me.
Zelda Philip, darling — how could I forget you? You silly man. (*Beat*) You
   were *first*.

A pause. Philip looks down, moved. Zelda takes his hand

   Close your eyes.
Philip Why?
Zelda Just do it.

*Philip closes his eyes. Zelda rises. She puts the pencil in his hand, kisses the
top of his head and picks up her rucksack*

   Now. Draw me.

   Zelda exits

Philip opens his eyes

Black-out

SCENE 6

The flat. The painting of Florence has disappeared from the wall

*Max emerges from Nina's room with two black plastic bags. He crosses the
room and exits. Nancy enters from the kitchen and stands for a moment, just
looking at the room. A beat, then Max re-enters*

Max Sunflowers are looking pretty good, Nance.
Nancy Oh! Aren't they. Some of them are taller than me.
Max Well — it's all spick and span, in there.
Nancy Oh, Max, you are good.
Max She left it pretty tidy, anyway. I just emptied the bin, hoovered round.
   Have you heard from her, yet?
Nancy Oh, she rings every night. Six o'clock sharp. I think it's habit, more

than anything. To tell me about her day. She seems cheerful, anyway. It sounds ever so nice. And where she's living sounds very smart. Very clean, she says.

Max Good. Long as she's happy. (*Beat*) So, you'll advertise, for the room?

Nancy I suppose so. I don't know. I'm not sure how I feel about it, some stranger moving in. I keep wondering if I shouldn't just sell up; get a one-bedroom sort of thing.

Max But you'll be all right, will you?

Nancy Oh yes, I'll be all right. (*Beat*) It was ever so quiet, when she first went. Silent. I put the washing-machine on spin, just for a bit of sound. Silly, isn't it? Yesterday I came over all emotional in Safeway, looking at all the things we used to slice down the middle. Funny, shopping for one. Makes you feel like half a person. Mind you, I buy that many packets of chocolate digestives, she'd go potty. (*Beat*) 'Course, we will see each other. I'm going up there in a couple of weeks, when she's settled in and she'll be down at Christmas. It's not like we won't be sisters any more, is it? (*Beat*) And I will miss her, Max. I do miss her. I even miss her shouting at me. But it's funny, you think you can't survive without someone. And then ... (*Beat*) You must miss her too.

Max Well, I do. But I always missed Nina, in a way. Even when she was there.

Nancy You've a lot of patience, Max.

Max Well, you've got to have patience if you love plants. Can't keep digging 'em up to see if they've grown yet, can you?

Nancy I feel like I've been *waiting* for as long as I can remember. Waiting for buses. Waiting in queues. Waiting for Sam Calder — d'you remember Sam, from my office? — for him to treat me to a lemonade shandy after work. Waiting for the oven to preheat, waiting for Nina to come home. (*Beat*) Only now, I don't know what I'm waiting for.

Max Seems to be life's all about waiting, Nance. And it's good to have something to wait for. Keeps you going. And you can wait for years, and even if you're waiting for the wrong thing, at least you've got something in mind. When you blow out a candle or chuck a coin in a fountain. Something to *want*. (*Beat*) See, I reckon most of what happens, day to day, most of it's just — warming the pot. Making yourself ready for the new. 'Cause nothing happens 'till you're ready. You've got to warm the pot before you can make the tea. (*Beat*) Why didn't you ever go out with Sam Calder, then? He was a decent fellow, Sam. Nice golfer, too. He was here a lot, at one time.

Nancy He did ask me, once. Just to go to the theatre, and for dinner. It was *The Mousetrap*. He won two tickets off a competition from *PG Tips*. I never went.

Max Why not?

Nancy You'll laugh if I tell you.
Max Laugh? Cross my heart, love, I won't even smile. Go on.
Nancy Well, it was because … It seems ever so daft, now.
Max What does?
Nancy Well, it was because, among other things, but mainly, it was because I was worried that I'd have to take ——
Max What?
Nancy No, never mind.
Max Ah, come on, take what?
Nancy Well — my clothes off.

A pause. Max tries very hard not to laugh. But, it's all right, because Nancy begins too laugh to. The laughter simply spills out if her, as she realizes the irony of what she's said. The laughter subsides. They look at each other

Max Right. I should be off. Leave you in peace.
Nancy Um, well. Actually. What I was going to say was, what I was thinking was, maybe you shouldn't. Be off, I mean. I mean, maybe you should stay.
Max Stay?
Nancy Yes. For tea.
Max Oh, for tea. Yes, well, tea would be lovely.

They smile at each other

Nancy And then, I was thinking. If tea goes well, maybe you might like to stay for supper. Maybe fish and chips, I thought.
Max I'd like that, Nance.
Nancy (*fast*) And then. And then we'd have to talk about what next. Because there's a room going free here, Max. And I know you like your independence, and you've got your routine and your greenhouse and everything, and I'm not Nina, after all …
Max No. You're Nancy. After all. (*Beat*) Be better than some stranger moving in, wouldn't it? I mean, I wouldn't worry about you, if I could be here.
Nancy There's a lot to talk about, isn't there, really.
Max There's a lot of time, though, Nance. All things considered.
Nancy Maybe we should just start with tea. What do you think? Start with tea and see how we get on.
Max Tea sounds perfect to me, love.

Nancy (*with a deep breath*) Let's just — warm the pot, then, shall we, Max? We'll warm the pot. And then we'll see.

They look at each other as the Lights fade

Black-out

THE END

FURNITURE AND PROPERTY LIST

ACT I

SCENE 1

On stage: Sofa
              Painting of Florence

Off stage: Two bags (**Nina**)
              Briefcase (**Nina**)

SCENE 2

On stage: as SCENE 1

Off stage: Tray of sunflower seedlings (**Max**)
              Pair of clip-on ear-rings (**Nina**)

SCENE 3

On stage: Raised plinth, draped in material

Personal: **Zelda**: cigarette

SCENE 4

On stage: as SCENE 1
              Jacket for **Max**
              Jar of pickled onions and a fork for **Nancy**

SCENE 5

On stage: Café table and chairs. *On **Philip**'s and **Zelda**'s table*: bowl with
                 sachets of sugar
              Paper and pen
              Bag for **Zelda**
              Notice-board

Off stage: Tray of tea

Personal: **Zelda**: Cigarettes and lighter

SCENE 6

On stage: Raised plinth
                Artists' easels and chairs. *On easels*: pencils and charcoal
                Tape-recorder
                Old-fashioned portable fire
                Arc lamp
                Wooden box and sharpener for **Luka**
                Jacket for *Philip*. *In it*: battered wallet with cheque book, pen

Off stage: Plastic bag (**Bridget**)
                Handbag containing lipstick and compact mirror (**Josie**)
                Sketch pad (**Martin**)
                Silk Chinese robe (**Nancy**)

Personal: **Sylvia**: tape

ACT II

SCENE 1

On stage: as ACT I, SCENE 1
                Envelope on front door mat

Off stage: Toolbox (**Max**)
                Planks of wood (**Max**)
                Two cups of tea (**Nina**)
                Plastic bag containing Tupperware box (**Nancy**)
                Cup of tea (**Nancy**)

SCENE 2

On stage: as ACT 1, SCENE 6
                Drawing board
                Paints and brushes for **Philip**

Off stage: Two plastic cups (**Philip**)

Personal: **Nancy**: Polo mints

SCENE 3

On stage: as SCENE 1

Off stage: Jar of pickled onions and fork (**Nina**)
                Two bottles of red wine
                Tray with two glasses and opened bottle of wine

Personal: **Nina**: Letter from SCENE 1

SCENE 4

On stage: Easel: *On easel*: oil painting of Nancy. Cloth covering
                Crash helmet for **Luka**

SCENE 5

On stage: Café table and chairs. *On table*: unfinished crossword puzzle
                Huge rucksack
                Pencil for **Philip**

SCENE 6

On stage: Sofa

Off stage: Two black plastic bags (**Max**)

LIGHTING PLOT

ACT 1

SCENE 1

To open: Darkness

Cue 1   When ready   (Page 1)
                       The Lights come up

Cue 2   **Nina:** " Why are you wearing your coat?"   (Page 2)
                       Black-out

SCENE 2

To open: General interior lighting

Cue 3   **Nancy** stares bleakly ahead   (Page 6)
                       Lights down

SCENE 3

To open: General interior lighting

Cue 4   **Zelda** hugs herself violently   (Page 7)
                       Black-out

SCENE 4

To open: General interior lighting

Cue 5   **Nina**: "And no-one's died."   (Page 10)
                       Black-out

SCENE 5

To open: General interior lighting

Cue 6   **Nancy** uncrumples a piece of paper and reads   (Page 14)
                       Black-out

Scene 6

To open: General interior lighting

Cue 7	**Philip** paces between easels murmuring instructions	(Page 25)
	Bring up spotlight on one side of the stage	

Cue 8	**Philip** switches on arc lamp	(Page 26)
	Bring up practical lamp	

ACT II

Scene 1

To open: Bright summery light fills the room

Cue 9	**Nancy** looks at **Nina** helplessly	(Page 30)
	Black-out	

Scene 2

To open: General interior lighting

Cue 10	**Nancy** and **Zelda** smile at each other	(Page 39)
	Black-out	

Scene 3

To open: General interior lighting

Cue 11	**Max** sits, lost in thought	(Page 45)
	Black-out	

Scene 4

To open: General interior lighting

Cue 12	The class gather around around **Nancy**	(Page 49)
	Black-out	

SCENE 5

To open: General interior lighting

Cue 13   **Philip** opens his eyes   (Page 51)
             Black-out

SCENE 6

To open: General interior lighting

Cue 14   **Max** and **Nancy** look at each other   (Page 53)
             Fade lights to black-out

EFFECTS PLOT

ACT 1

Cue 1   As Scene 2 opens   (Page 2)
              The doorbell rings

Cue 2   **Philip** bounds up from the tape recorder   (Page 25)
              A piece of very beautiful classical music begins to play

ACT II

Cue 3   **Nancy**: "Well in the art class —"   (Page 30)
              Max *begins to hammer in the bathroom*

Cue 4   **Nina** paces eating pickled onions   (Page 39)
              The doorbell rings